LEVEL
1

Predator Face-Off

Melissa Stewart

NATIONAL GEOGRAPHIC

Washington, D.C.

For Laura, Kathryn, and Shelby, editors extraordinaire —M.S.

The author and publisher gratefully acknowledge the expert content review of this book by Bill Swanson, Ph.D., director of animal research, Center for Conservation and Research of Endangered Wildlife, Cincinnati Zoo, and the literacy review of this book by Mariam Jean Dreher, professor of reading education, University of Maryland, College Park.

Author's Note: All kinds of predators live on Earth. This book invites young readers to compare and contrast three predators that belong to different animal groups (fish, mammal, reptile), live in different environments (ocean, savanna, forest), and hunt in different ways.

The title page photo shows a great white shark coming out of the water. The photo on the Table of Contents page shows a king cobra with its hood extended. This makes the snake look bigger to its enemies.

Photo Credits:
AL: Alamy Stock Photo; GI: Getty Images; NPL: Nature Picture Library; SS: Shutterstock

Cover (UP), vladoskan/GI; (CTR), Ben Cartland/GI; (LO), suebg1 photography/GI; page border (throughout): (snake), HuHu/SS; (cheetah), AKorolchuk/SS; (shark), Airin.dizain/SS; vocabulary box (throughout), Ken Cook/SS; 1 (CTR), NPL/AL; 3 (LO RT), Eric Isselée/SS; 4 (LO), Carlos Villoch-MagicSea.com/AL; 5 (UP), Stuart G. Porter/SS; 5 (LO), Michael and Patricia Fogden/Minden Pictures; 6–7 (CTR), wildestanimal/GI; 8–9 (CTR), 3DMI/SS; 10 (CTR), BW Folsom/SS; 10 (LO), Martin Prochazkacz/SS; 11 (UP), B Christopher/AL; 12–13 (UP), Andy Rouse/NPL; 14–15 (CTR), Eric Isselée/SS; 16 (CTR), ZSSD/Minden Pictures; 17 (LO), Keith Lewis Hull England/GI; 18 (CTR), WaterFrame/AL; 19 (UP), Image Source/AL; 19 (CTR), Bertie Gregory/NPL; 19 (LO), Anyka/AL; 20 (CTR), Jim Cumming/GI; 21 (CTR), David Kleyn/AL; 22–23 (CTR), Patrick K. Campbell/SS; 22 (LE), Jim Cumming/GI; 24 (CTR), Jim Cumming/GI; 25 (CTR), Papilio/AL; 26 (UP), Matthijs Kuijpers/AL; 26 (LO), reptiles4all/SS; 27 (CTR), Eric Isselée/Dreamstime; 28 (LO), Mark Conlin/AL; 29 (CTR), Kim Taylor/NPL/GI; 30 (LO LE), Jeff Rotman/GI; 30 (LO RT), Valdecasas/SS; 31 (UP LE), Elsa Hoffman/SS; 31 (UP RT), imageBROKER/AL; 31 (LO LE), reptiles4all/SS; 31 (LO RT), Andre Coetzer/SS; 32 (UP LE), Jim Abernethy/GI; 32 (UP RT), Federico Veronesi/GI; 32 (LO LE), ephotocorp/AL; 32 (LO RT), reptiles4all/SS

Library of Congress Cataloging-in-Publication Data

Names: Stewart, Melissa, author.
Title: Predator face-off / Melissa Stewart.
Description: Washington, DC : National Geographic, [2017] | Series: National Geographic readers | Audience: Ages 4-6. | Audience: K to grade 3.
Identifiers: LCCN 2016051333 (print) | LCCN 2017009785 (ebook) | ISBN 9781426328114 (pbk. : alk. paper) | ISBN 9781426328121 (hardcover : alk. paper) | ISBN 9781426328138 (e-book) | ISBN 9781426328145 (e-book + audio)
Subjects: LCSH: Predatory animals--Juvenile literature. | Predation (Biology)--Juvenile literature.
Classification: LCC QL758 .S7425 2017 (print) | LCC QL758 (ebook) | DDC591.5/3--dc23
LC record available at https://lccn.loc.gov/2016051333

National Geographic supports K–12 educators with ELA Common Core Resources. Visit natgeoed.org/commoncore for more information.

Printed in the United States of America
19/WOR/4

Table of Contents

What's a Predator?

Great white sharks swim in the sea.
Cheetahs run across the land.
Parrot snakes slide along tree
branches.

They are very different. But they
all eat meat.

These animals are predators
(PRED-uh-ters).

Word Bite

PREDATOR: An animal that hunts other animals for food

cheetah

parrot snake

great white shark

Shark Attack!

A great white shark
spots a seal. It darts up
and crashes into its prey.
Chomp! The shark
takes a big bite.
It swims in a circle.
Then it starts
to eat.

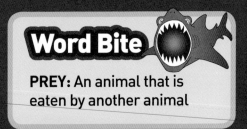

Word Bite

PREY: An animal that is
eaten by another animal

A great white shark is the size of a pickup truck. It's one of the biggest fish in the world. And its body is built to hunt.

TAIL: Pushes the shark through the water at up to 25 miles an hour

SKIN: Feels ripples when animals move in the water

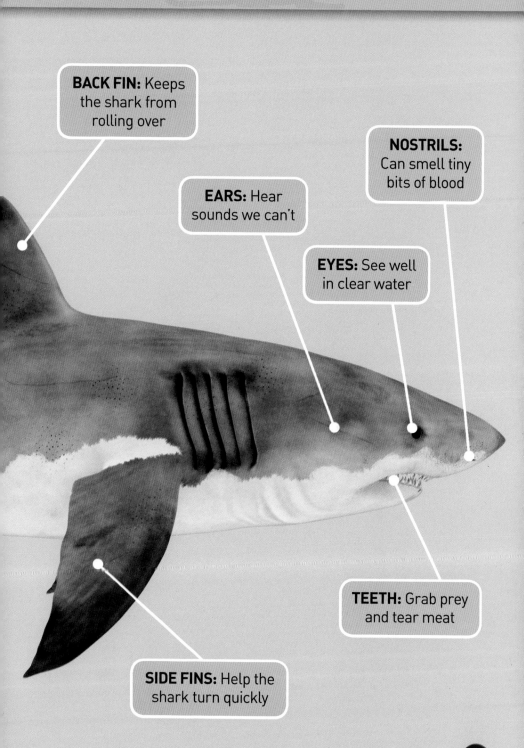

BACK FIN: Keeps the shark from rolling over

EARS: Hear sounds we can't

NOSTRILS: Can smell tiny bits of blood

EYES: See well in clear water

TEETH: Grab prey and tear meat

SIDE FINS: Help the shark turn quickly

How many teeth does a great white shark use at once? About 50.

shark teeth

Q What do you call the stuff stuck between a shark's teeth?

A Slow swimmers.

This photo shows the teeth and jaw on a great white shark skeleton.

Each tooth will wear out. Then the one behind it takes its place. A shark may use 20,000 teeth in its life.

Run, Cheetah, Run

Shh! A cheetah slinks through the grass. It creeps closer and closer to a gazelle (guh-ZELL).

The cheetah leaps. The chase is on!

Thud! The predator knocks the gazelle to the ground and bites its neck.

Time to eat.

13

Cheetahs are wild cats. They live in the grasslands of Africa.

How does a cheetah's body help it hunt? Take a look.

TAIL: Helps with balance during quick turns

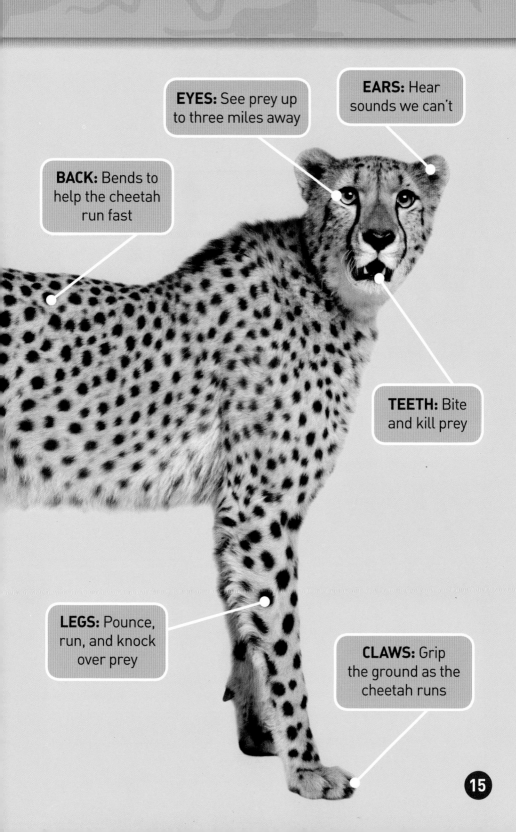

EYES: See prey up to three miles away

EARS: Hear sounds we can't

BACK: Bends to help the cheetah run fast

TEETH: Bite and kill prey

LEGS: Pounce, run, and knock over prey

CLAWS: Grip the ground as the cheetah runs

15

Cheetahs are the fastest animals on land. They can run more than 60 miles an hour—but not for long.

They have to slow down after about 20 seconds.

The Need for Speed

Are cheetahs the only fast predators on Earth? No way! Lots of animals use speed to get food.

A mantis shrimp breaks open a clam shell with its claws. It can punch through water at 50 miles an hour.

A sailfish can swim up to 68 miles an hour. It uses its super speed to catch smaller fish.

A peregrine (PEAR-eh-gren) falcon dives to catch smaller birds. It can travel up to 200 miles an hour.

A chameleon (kuh-MEEL-yun) has a quick tongue. It can grab an insect faster than you can blink your eyes.

It's a Snake!

A parrot snake flicks its tongue.
In. Out. In. Out.

Finally, it picks up a scent. Tree frog!

The snake winds through the trees.
Then it spots the prey. It darts
forward and grabs the frog.

Dinnertime!

21

EYES: See well during the day

SKIN: Stretches when the snake swallows prey

TONGUE: Smells the air for prey

TEETH: Grab prey

THIN BODY: Doesn't get stuck on branches

The parrot snake lives in Central America and South America. It makes its home in forests. Its body is perfect for hunting in trees.

Word Bite

SCUTES: The wide scales on a snake's belly

SCUTES: Grip tree bark so the snake won't fall

A parrot snake has 36 small teeth. They can grab prey. But they can't chew.

How does the snake swallow prey?

1 It stretches its mouth over the prey.

 2 It pulls back the jaws on one side of its head.

 3 It pulls back the jaws on the other side of its head.

4 Slowly. Slowly. The prey slides into the snake's mouth and down its throat.

Snakes With Venom

The inland taipan has the deadliest venom. Just one drop can kill a person.

Most snakes hunt like a parrot snake. But some snakes make venom. It flows into prey through two large fangs.

fangs

The Great Lakes bush viper has huge fangs, but its venom isn't strong enough to kill a person.

The king cobra is the biggest snake with venom. It usually eats other snakes.

Word Bite

VENOM: A liquid that some snakes use to hurt or kill other animals

27

All Kinds of Predators

Sharks. Wild cats. Snakes.

They're just a few of the predators that share our world.

A sea star has strong legs. They can pry open a clam's shell. What a tasty treat!

It's easy to guess how a jumping spider catches its prey. Pounce!

Predators live in many different places. And they hunt in all kinds of ways.

What in the World?

These pictures show close-up views of predators. Use the hints below to figure out what's in the pictures.

Answers are on page 31.

1

HINT: It keeps a shark from rolling over.

2

HINT: A cheetah uses these to grip the ground.

Word Bank

peregrine falcon   back fin   fangs   claws   tongue   teeth

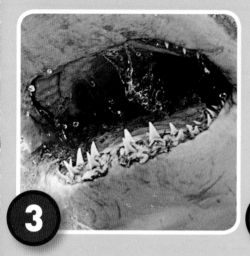

3

HINT: A shark uses 20,000 of these in its life.

4

HINT: This predator can dive 200 miles an hour.

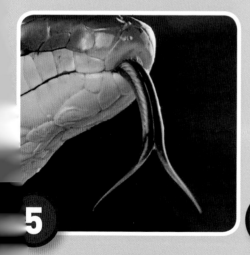

5

HINT: A snake uses it to smell.

6

HINT: Venom flows through these.

Answers: 1. back fin, 2. claws, 3. teeth, 4. peregrine falcon, 5. tongue, 6. fangs

PREDATOR: An animal that hunts other animals for food

PREY: An animal that is eaten by another animal

SCUTES: The wide scales on a snake's belly

VENOM: A liquid that some snakes use to hurt or kill other animals